Two Barks

poems by
JULIE O'CALLAGAN

illustrated by
MARTIN FISH

BLOODAXE BOOKS

ISBN: 1 85224 427 5

First published 1998 by
Bloodaxe Books Ltd,
P.O. Box 1SN,
Newcastle upon Tyne NE99 1SN.

Bloodaxe Books Ltd acknowledges
the financial assistance of Northern Arts.

Cover printing by J. Thomson Colour Printers Ltd, Glasgow.

Printed in Great Britain by
Cromwell Press Ltd, Trowbridge, Wiltshire.

*For my
brothers and sisters*

ACKNOWLEDGEMENTS

Acknowledgements are due to the editors of the following publications where some of these poems first appeared: *Casting a Spell* (Orchard Books, 1991), *Children's Books in Ireland*, *The Irish Times* and *Stopping for Death* (Viking, 1996). 'Jasper the Lion Heart' appeared in a limited edition from Gefn Press, London.

Thanks are also due to the Irish Arts Council/An Chomhairle Ealaion for a children's writing bursary.

CONTENTS

Air

Call me in.
I'm on my bicycle
lost in the neighbourhood
under the trees
waiting for someone
to call me
through the air
which I count on
to hold me up.

My Life

Look at it coming
down the street
toward us:
it chokes me up
every time I see it
walking along
all by itself.
How does it know
for example
which corner
is the right one
to turn at?
Who tells it
to keep going
past the intersection
and take the first left
after the supermarket?
There it goes –
I'll follow quietly
and see where
it's off to.

Buying Your Voice

I want to buy your voice.
There is a kiosk
down the street
where it is sold.
I've been saving up
for a while to have it.

You will hear me paying for it
in California, Kate,
and we will blab
to the value of ten pounds.
When the last coin has been used
the machine will bleep
and no matter how loudly we scream
no sound will come through.

All You Want To Do

Someday you will tell your mother:
    'So sorry – I don't want to visit
    the children's art exhibit.'
To your father you will explain:
    'If you don't mind, I'll give that
    young person's concert a miss.'
When the doorbell rings, say:
    'Thanks anyway, but I'm not in the mood
    for pancakes and kite-flying.'
Supposing your friend invites you, reply:
    'There's no ice-skating and doughnuts
    for me today – maybe I can go next week.'
If it's your cousin on the phone, try:
    'Have fun at the movies,
    don't throw popcorn at the screen.'

                All you want to do
                is sit in the kitchen
                twirling spaghetti
                onto a fork
                and after that
                to stop at the window
                as if watching for snow.

Babysitting

They say they will
    clean up the house and fix the TV
        if only I will come
            and watch their young.

They say the kiddies
    will be in pyjamas
        and will fall asleep as I arrive
            so will I please, please babysit?

They want to know which I prefer: Coke or Pepsi
    and am I allergic to poodles or gerbils
        and, if I mind changing Pampers, it's OK.
            So, have I decided?

They will order a pizza and get in pretzels
    and I can phone anyone in the world
        and they'll pay double after midnight
            if only I'll say yes!

I tell them I'll think about it.

The #22 Clark Street Bus

We packed jars of Gerber Baby Food
(banana and apricot mush)
threw in ham and mustard sandwiches
(not forgetting peanut-butter-and-jelly-ones)
and a bag of Jays potato chips –
it was a picnic!
We began munching slowly
on the #22 Clark Street Bus.
'Everyone gets one more potato chip –
then we eat the rest at the park.'
We didn't allow younger kids to run up and down
or stick their heads out the window.
Everybody sat still and wiped
beads of sweat off their top lip.
Where in the world was that park?
'Keep your shirt on –
we'll be there in a while.'
Nobody could kick or pinch.
'Look at all this stuff passing by.'
If you could smell the zoo,
you got off the bus,
grabbed the brown paper bags
like crazy and ran over
to a wonderful picnic place
beside some ducks
and a fountain.

Riding the Elevated

Riding the elevated when you're young
is riding to a matinee or ballet class.
Every time you pass the street you live on
you try to see your house, but you never do.

Then you watch the tops of cars
and backs of buildings, look into rooms
of apartments a few inches away.
A little boy will always be waving.

When you're older, you don't look out –
you hate going to work and you're tired.
You bring a paper wall with words on it
to set up all around you.

Or you yawn and file your nails,
nothing will surprise you – you've ridden
the elevated train for twenty-eight years
armed with a handbag for every eventuality.

Kate, Me, Metal Turtle Clicker

Do you see two girls' heads
up at the diamond-paned windows?
That's us.
When a lady click-clacks by our house
we press the stomach
of our metal turtle clicker,
so each time she takes a step
we add to the sound effects.
She leans against our picket fence,
checks the bottom of her shoes
to find out what's making such a racket.

'Oh darn,' she thinks, 'I bet I lost
the rubber heel off my stilettos.'
Up in our window at midnight
we control who does
and who does not tippy-tap.
Kate and I rule on hot nights.
In our attic look-out
we lick popsicles thoughtfully,
dangle our feet on the ledge
and decide.

The Glass

of juice
is at my mouth.
I peer down its telescope
past the orange liquid,
past my hand
and, far far off,
find my younger face
looking back through time.
Watch me at the table
with the glass up to my mouth.
My mother is asking me
what I find so interesting
inside that glass.
I hear as if through a set
of tin-can phones joined with string.
The girl inside my glass
doesn't know I can see her.
She laughs when people ask her
what she stares at.
I swallow the juice
and she runs away.

Design

I wanted to organise
my life into
a pattern.

Red socks and
a striped hairbow
on Wednesdays.

For a humdrum Tuesday,
spearmint gum
and a book about horses.

Saturdays, all I'd need
were tassels on my shoes
and a lace butterfly pin.

The way I felt
about Sunday
called for a white

linen dress and straw
hat, a story
about a river adventure.

Tornado

Nana calls up
and says, 'Get everyone inside,
a twister's on its way.'
I think to myself:
if a twister's on its way,
why hide? How are you supposed to know
where it is
unless you sit on the porch
and watch for it?
You could be crouching
in the basement for days
and unless you had a periscope
you'd be none the wiser.
'Okey doke, Nana, I'll pull them all in.
You just keep calm and say hi to Pop.'

On the porch we sat in green light
and the stillest, thinnest air.
We were not near a train line
but, if we heard a train coming,
it was time to pack our bags.

Pumpkinhead

If I stand at our fence
I can watch my brother
setting off for school.
It took him all last night
to carve the pumpkin on his head.
From here, he looks hilarious
with that huge orange head
and a flowing white sheet
covering the rest of him.
He carries his book-bag
just like any other school day
and walks along humming,
up to the bus stop.
Will he sit on the bus
with a pumpkin on his head?
Yes, he will.
He'll live inside there all day –
he measured the grinning mouth
and it is big enough
to pass a spoon and fork
and a candy bar into.
I lean over our fence
but he's just a little orange dot.

Communion Dress

Pleat pearl – pearl pleat
in delicate rows
down the front.
My mom saying
'Isn't this one pretty?'
(it never was).
After the pleats and pearls
a sash or something
tied in a bow at the back.
A skirt that stuck out
the way it was supposed to,
I suppose.
Do you understand a lace veil?
It was on my head
except when I used it as a cape.
A saint praying
with sad eyes.
You put your hands
in a holy posture
and your thumbs
formed a cross
only God could see,
fingertips indicating
the direction of heaven.
I offered up my black
clodhopper tie-shoes
for the poor souls.

Dude Ranch

You are sitting on a suitcase
at a moist hot train station
in the jungle of Indiana.

You have been here, by your reckoning,
which at this point tends to elephantitis,
for a million years.

You try your hardest not to look
like a lost orphan with nowhere to go
in this heartless world.

You don't want to cry but tears
are lurking as the shadows grow
and no one comes to pick you up.

You pretend you don't notice
the housewife across the tracks
until, miraculously, she calls to you.

You tell her where you're aimed
and she goes inside, shaking her head,
to make a phone call.

You give the cowpoke in the red sports car
and ten gallon hat a filthy look
when he helps you into the front seat.

He's awfully sorry about the mix-up,
but the folks at the Triple R Dude Ranch
are just busting to meet me.

Poetry Soup

It is coming slowly to the boil,
the soup of poetry.
I stir it, poke my finger in it,
check for seasoning.
Could it be more creamy?
I look down into the pot
and daydream in soup-orbits,
rings of years, bubbles.
Ladles of steam.
The noodles of my life floating
through the bowl of time!
Pick up that spoon and slurp.

Legs

Are you all here?
It's that time
of the wide brook
in Wisconsin.
The station wagon
will be crusted
in sand crystals.
All of us will
ride home covered
in magic dust
just like usual.
So many legs.

A Weekend

in October when the clocks change
to wintertime passes so fast
I hardly notice the red trees –
it gets dark too suddenly.
I wish it was summer.
The sky hasn't got the hang
of sunsets at 5 yet.
He keeps a pinkish blue up
until the darkness whispers at him
from the wings
that the show's over early tonight.

Then the sky remembers
and for a finale
stands on its head with violet.
An October twilight in the universe.
I'm moody and it's raining.
I wish it was July.

Learning Can Be Fun!

Lounging around the kitchen
after school can be rewarding.

Don't look now, but I think I see
the makings of a science project
growing on a furry tomato.

Let's hope electrical heat conduction,
the chemistry of baking powder, eggs and flour,
the physics of rising matter
and the mathematics of batter
plus heat plus time equals cake.

While waiting, you commence
an experiment to discover
the cubic capacity of the human stomach.

Four O'Clocks

red canvas gym shoes
white rubber toes and soles
playing in the grass
at the side of the house
a grasshopper a worm a cricket
sitting next to the water spout
waiting for the four o'clocks to open
it's almost four she said
don't pull the petals
Max was a puppy then
chewing grass chasing squirrels
a man has gone up
our front porch stairs with tools
to repair the refrigerator
he looks stinky and hot
Max put her paw on my arm
and snapped at my nose
I pushed her away and she squeaked
maybe bunnies lived
under the wooden front porch
like under Mr Brownlee's
rickety lopsided porch
a bicycle stood on its head
with both ferris wheels revolving
a 25A bus slouched by towards Ashland Avenue
sometimes we rode that bus the other way
to the Grenada cinema
a golden palace of cartoons and *Milk Duds*
is it four o'clock yet
are the flowers open
no
well then it's not four o'clock is it
what time is it then
kiiiids I'm going to Jewel

answer the phone and don't fight
pulling off a bandaid
the breeze carried her perfume
who's watching that man
what if he eats our fudgicles
he won't – leave that alone
Max bit my hair – ouch that hurt
the baby threw her rattle
I'm telling Mom you said that
the bicycle fell over
tattle-tale
ants climbing up a stem
carrying crumbs
go in and see if any fudgicle wrappers
are in the garbage
not without camouflage I won't
he lowered his Batman mask
over his eyes and went inside
holding the ends of his cape
don't do that to the poor ant
mind your own beeswax
I made two loops of cotton shoe string
and knotted them
pulling one side of the bow smaller
so each loop was perfect
not like the Nolans
they use only one loop
he didn't eat any – or else
he hid the evidence in his pocket
what's he doing
unscrewing something underneath
the baby's eating mush
finger in gob
pull out paper
you're supposed to be watching her
I'm answering the phone
a petal moved

I wouldn't mind so much
if we had wild kittens
like last year
we made a box trap
with a bowl of milk
a stick and a long string
but we couldn't catch anything
bunnies don't arch their backs at you
let's pretend this isn't really
our house and that we
can't understand English
Nancy wants to talk to you on the phone
bye kids tell your mom
the fridge is A-OK now
we stared at him
and ran to the kitchen
to see how many fudgicles were left
the baby drooled
and whacked Max's tail with her fist
what time is it
I forgot about the flowers

At My Desk

Sunbeam on the wall,
get lost.
I can't go out and have fun.
I can't go out and be warm.
I can't go out and see the sights.
Stop coming in my window
making me want things
I can't have.

Hurrah – Morning

I don't wake up gracefully.
I fall out of bed
into a pile of yesterday's clothes
which I keep there
so as not to crack my skull
into smithereens – ouch.
Well then, blah, blah,
I eat a bowl of horse feed
and I get my face
stuck into a glass of milk
whilst annoying my sister
by swinging my leg
scientifically back and forth
almost skimming her shins.
I get a kick out of screaming.
It clears my thoughts
for the busy day ahead.
I toss myself onto this jolly
old orange school bus
and greet my school chums.
Do they return my greeting?
No, they do not – those rats.
They are listening to Iron Maiden
on their headsets.
Oh gee, I wonder what life
has in store for me today?

Nasty Asteroid

I dream of the six-mile-wide
asteroid that will collide
with the earth in 2115.

The sky tonight is powder blue
as if sugar stars
wouldn't melt in its mouth.

So quiet up there.
So hectic down here.
While we play, it's falling.

While we open a letter, it's coming.
As we change the Walkman batteries
it's on its way.

The Great Attractor

Everyone in the Universe
(including all of you flapjaws
up on Saturn and you lounge lizards
over there on Jupiter)
is going: it's like
an intergalactic field trip.
The Milky Way big-wigs
will be handing out name tags
and tee-shirts so we won't
get lost in the crowd.
Since all known matter
and lots of other
solar systems are going,
we want to cut a dash.
Just because The Great Attractor
out there in eternity
is pulling us towards it
at 250 miles per hour
and looks like a big black hole,
is no reason
to get down in the dumps!
We'll be starting a rollicking sing-song
before too many light years pass
and don't forget to cast your satellite vote
on which Hollywood Classic you'd like
as our in-flight movie along the way.

An Astronaut Looks at the Moon

It is late, my children,
and time for bed –
but before you go,
come over to the window
with your dear old dad
and look up in the sky
at the floating moon.
When I was on the moon,
I gazed at the earth
as if from a boat,
seeing where I lived
from a new angle.
I bounced up and down on the moon.
I swung a golf club.
I picked up moon dust.
Do you see me, kids?
There haven't been many men
on the moon with a dinky spacecraft
like a cozy camper to sleep in.
When I peeked out
in the lunar morning
I was the man in the moon.
Let's pretend we're on the moon
and over there – that globe –
is the earth with millions of people
you've never met and never will.
That's what it's like.
It's lonely as anything.

Food for a Storm

For lightning, the electric onion
will never fail you.

For swelling seas, day-old
bread mixed with herbs.

During hurricane winds, boil rice noodles
or, if gale, egg noodle.

Are you quaking with fear?
Bring out the potatoes for dampness.

Stun the garlic clove
if hail marbles rattle.

Cube a tomato and sprinkle with dill
but only after the first thunder clap.

Come out from under that dresser
and whip these eggs for storm stamina.

As to the full-arch rainbow,
that is the time for puff pastry.

Pets Pets Pets

My guinea pig bit me
so I sort of hate it now
because I ran around
getting it crisp lettuce
and crunchy carrots
and then it does that!

And the kitten was cute:
we laughed when it
batted its paw at a string.
It was so soft and pretty
but then it sank its claws in my hand –
I wonder why it did.

I loved my red finches.
They tweeted and I took care
of them, filled their seed tray,
gave them tasty fruit.
They never bothered anyone.
Look at them there, feet up.

Then again, Rex the dog is wacky.
He pulls us down the street
and hides in certain places
at our house to sleep.
We put baseball hats on him
and he doesn't mind at all.

My horse loves the beach, oats,
hay, apples and listening.
When you ride him he wants to run
to find out where we're going –
in between his brown ears
you will see my goofy face.

Conchita and Pepito

It is thus –
they are Conchita and Pepito
my chihuahua comrades.
Buenos dias, my doggitos!

Are you well?
How have you slept?
Dreaming of the chase
and noble adventures?

Come along, Pepito,
let us see your skill
at play-acting:
firstly show us

the wounded–paw walk.
How deeply moving!
Conchita, you are the nurse –
examine poor Pepito's paw

and wrap it in a bandage.
Bravely done, mi amiga.
Take a break, small ones,
before we begin our dancing.

Here are your sombreros
and spangled costumes
in tip-top condition
for the performance.

Do not growl at each other,
my children, there are
dog biscuits for all.
Two barks, now, for luck.

Girl in Tin Photograph

I've been squashed
inside this leather book
for one hundred years.

If you search for the porch
I'm standing on
you'll find it.

After you're finished
talking about my muslin dress
and huge hairbow

and have stopped tapping
this tin picture
and joking around,

blow the dust
off my face.
Leave me in peace.

Sad Faces in the Border

In the garden, the plants
are begging me,
they are pleading,
their stalks are reaching,
imploring, they are
on their knees,
hands joined over heads,

praying to anyone
anywhere with clout
to send them – and soon –
just the weakest ray
the milkiest stream
the teeniest megawatt
of sunshine.

Then they would bloom
and change colours
and raise their heads up high,
dance and throw a barbeque.
It would be a total blast.
I avoid eye-contact with them,
cover my ears.

Polka Dots

Supposing you buy a tortoiseshell hairband
for twenty bucks in Henri Bendel's.
A girl in Chanel and pearls
wraps it in the finest shocking-pink paper.
She whips out a dinky black
lacquered power-shopping carrier bag
with Henri's name discreetly emblazoned.
Does she shove the pink-wrapped
twenty buck purchase in without more ado?

She leans over and produces several sheets
of festive polka dot tissue paper
and artistically flutes the edges.
She lines the bag so that the polka dots
are visible from all angles,
drops your merchandise in,
ties a bow on the handles
and presents you with
your very own fashion statement.

I Hate the Ocean

It's roaring down at the end of our street.
It threw a wave on top of me today.
I hate it more than anything.
I hate it more than liver.
It drenched my head
and made me
choke.
If you look at the horizon it's bumpy.
That's how you get dizzy and sick.
It's noisy, sloppy and stinks.
What's to admire about it?
It's always in my way.
That lousy old
sea.

Green

Soon
I will find a use
for all the green
inside me.
I will draw it out
of my head
and a garland
of leaves and plants
and everything that sprouts
outside this window
will come tumbling
from my ears.
The more I pull
the greener
my memories
will look.

Winter Festival

I *Carol*

That time was winter.
How many alleluias
had they chanted since midnight?
On the refectory table,
God had granted them
butter, honey, plump apples –
and, under it, cold sandalled feet.
Each tried to be joyful –
breath hung in a halo over their heads.
As they ate, an angel appeared
with a golden harp
playing festive carols.
Turf was heaped on the fire.
Beakers lifted.

II *Nollaig*

Something outside is singing:
wood pigeon, robin, storm.
Our holiday comes gift-wrapped in clouds,
the most beautiful shades of grey
and, if we are good, a display
of tinsel rain will fall
(no two drops alike).
Down hedge-boreens at midnight,
the wren watches a man in red,
a cart pulled by jingling heifers.
Light the candle –
listen for singing in the chimney.

III *Turn the Handle*

Once I turn the handle
I am in the dream-time-zone of winter
yakking about happy festive topics
while pushing beautiful cakes
carefully between my choppers.
Robins hop out of harp notes
holding tinsel in their beaks
for the chandelier.
I make the acquaintance
of a large spruce tree
loaded down with baubles and gauds:
its needles point toward
the glittering snowdrift
at the base of the french doors.
I toss a frozen bombe into my gullet.
Sparklers explode from my ears.
The man sporting a holly wreath around his neck
has called for a game of charades.
If you are a Christmas Mummer,
crawl out from under the piano.
You are granted only one
spangled room in your life.
Turn the handle.
Step inside.

The Dress

My sister says,
'Just ask them –
they'll buy it for you.'
The dress waiting for me downtown
on a plastic hanger
is sick of the Junior Miss Department
and would love to go to a few parties.

But I remember the flowing white streamer
a mile long my mother is handed
at the supermarket each Saturday –
I figure they can't afford it.
'Tell them you'll clean the house,
take out the garbage
and wash the dishes for a year.'

Oh maybe I *can* talk them into it.
I go downstairs to try.

Hair with Zing

Oh every knucklebrain
knows you need hair with ZING
in this life or you can forget it.
Do you have a problem with that?

Braids, bows, bobs –
do they freak you out?
Go get your head examined –
they will trim it off for you
or pick up a strand and say:
'What have you done to this?'
Hand over your head – give in.

We all dream of hair with oomph,
hair that will make mouths drop,
curls that couldn't possibly be
a stinky perm, shimmering golden ringlets.
Hold your locks up high –
walk forth into the future
of heavenly hair-dos.

Mr Potato Head

When you stop that dumb-bell
show-off act, I'll let you see
the Mr Potato Head game I've brought.
It's for you.
Here's a potato: stick in the eyes –
make it look funny for goodness sake.
You can have it look nutty too,
just put the ears on upside down.
Don't you want to have fun?
Well if you do, go ahead and have some.
There are zillions of zany faces you can shape.
Try making him look like a monster
with these prominent teeth.
He's got a cute blue hat –
why not include it?
It matches his blue moustache.
Get over here and play.

Three Children from Brueghel Paintings

I *Numbering at Bethlehem*

That was the first day I ever felt lonely.
Our cottage was cold and damp,
my mother busy with housework,
my brothers and sisters
outside with their friends.
No one cared about me
so I put on my coat
and walked over the shivering fields
to where the kids around here
play on the frozen river.
Well, I was in a rotten mood
to begin with, but when I saw
everyone through a frosty haze
skating, sledding, spinning tops,
shouting and laughing on the ice
I felt alone in the world.
Nobody called, 'Johann, come on out
and pull my sled' or 'Johann, I bet
I can spin a top faster than you'
or 'Get your skates and I'll race you'.
It was as though I had died
and stood like a ghost
watching the snowy afternoon
from the afterlife.

II *Hunters in the Snow*

This is the agreement:
I pull you to your house
and you pull me to mine – OK?
Whoever is pulling has to make sure
that we don't slide
on any weak spots in the ice
and the horse has to trot a little
because it's not such fun
if you're riding on a sled
and the horse is just walking
all the time – is it?
The horse can have only one
resting stop and shouldn't spend
the whole trip moaning
about how slippery the ice is
and how heavy the passenger is.
If the horse goes over a bumpy area
and the sled capsizes
the passenger gets another ride free
to wherever she wants to go.
Since I thought up all the rules,
I will be the first-ever passenger.
You can start acting like a nag now.

111 *The Wedding Feast*

My sister is the bride today.
I carried the ring into the church
and scattered rose petals on the way out.
Yesterday she chased our peacock
all around the yard
before she plucked
one of its tail feathers for my hat.
I wish I could have brought
my friend to the wedding –
I wanted her to see me in my
new dress, best apron and fancy hat.
They said I'm allowed to stay up
until the dancing is almost over.
It isn't fair that I have to sit
on the floor and get all dusty.
I've hidden a few pieces of cake
in a secret pocket for my friend.
From now on, I have a room to myself
and my sister's husband will have to listen
to all her bossy blather – not me!

Calculation

Let's assume that today,
in Dublin,
it is summer.
If we then call the wind 'X'
and the rain 'Y'
and the clouds 'W'
and the puddles 'O'
we can begin to calculate
the relationship
between Irish summers
and good weather.
Our equation
would look something like this:

$$\frac{XxYxW+O}{Summer} = \text{not very long.}$$

Run outside – quick!

46

Nun About to Sneeze

A nun is hunting for her pockets
in folds and pleats and flaps
of black material.
There is a twinge
in her right nostril
which alerts her hands
to start the search.
'Jesus, Mary and Joseph',
she thinks to herself,
'What in the world
have I done with my handkerchief?'
Thirty-two little girls
follow her frantic movements
up under there by her cross
or beside her holy medal
or near her scapular
while she explains multiplication.
The nun is producing something
out of somewhere the girls
cannot imagine in a million years.
She brings her hands to her nose
and blows the foghorn.
She wipes and blows again.
She sniffles and her ring glitters.
But the girls in her class
never will understand
how to multiply.

Autumn

I defoil a piece of sugarless gum.
I fold it into three
and deposit in gob.
The world smells of smoked ham.
The leaves are supposed to be dying
but all around my head
perfectly healthy foliage
is whacking into me.
While chewing, I fix my gaze
on the hedgehog manse to my right.
I can almost hear them snoring.
What's with that bunch? –
You give them milk and bread
and they ignore it.
I like donkeys better –
they don't keep hiding all the time.
Shove a carrot at their mouth
and they're happy – I wish someone
would hand one to the donkey braying
a few blocks away.
I'm trying to watch
the ribs of the sky
in peace.

Jasper the Lion Heart

My fingers grip like paws.
I stare at my hand
and say to myself:
'Once I sharpened claws
on tree bark.

It was the dream-time
before I became a boy.
Now I must hide that life.'
I wore a cape of tufted fur then.
Look at me.

Here is a striped sweater.
It fits over my head
with two tunnels for my arms.
God of the Jungle, forgive this human
who tells me she's my mother.

How is she to know our ways?:
how we never wear another's pelt,
how a sheep's wool is not suitable
for a boy with a lion heart?
I roar and roar and roar.

But she speaks another language.
My call makes her laugh.
My earlier mother would have
picked me up by the neck
in her sharp gentle teeth.

Where have those times gone?
I wish to growl deeply
as my lion-father once did
with jaws wide and jagged
and powerful as a sprung trap.

I roar at alleyways and shadows.
I roar at the shelves of toys in my room.
I roar when my human mother
tells me the neighbours will be frightened
and think there is a wild animal here.

Inside my head I stalk gazelle
and sleep on tree branches
and roll on my back in the sun.
How did this mix-up happen?
I swipe at wooden blocks

with my weak boy-hand
and show my milky teeth
to the stuffed polar bear.
If I were a lion
it would all make sense.

But that life is over.
I will wait in my room
with these toys.
Who can say what
I will turn into next?

GRRRRRRRRRRRRRRRRRRRRR.

Back in Ten Minutes

If you'll excuse me,
I must now quit writing
and walk down a street
you probably never even heard of
called Dempster.
It should take me five minutes
to arrive at the corner
of Dempster and Chicago Avenue.
Then I will push open
the glass door of *31 Flavors Ice Cream*
and inform the assistant
that a Boysenberry and Daiquiri Ice
double-dip on a sugar-cone
would be the perfect combination for me.
I'll grip that cone tightly,
licking the drippy stuff
and return the way I came.
I can finish this poem later...

If It's Raining

on a dark September afternoon,
stick your head
inside an ivy bush
growing on an old wall.
A blackbird will be sitting
in a green room
singing about worms.
In a crack
a striped snail
is dozing – getting ready
for a busy night
of chewing.
The ivy loves how she looks
when raindrops polish up her leaves.
She has plans
about where to spread
her new shoots.

Why Cry?

You know something wonderful
will always happen.
It always does.
Know what I mean?
Like how
you just opened the window
and the warm breeze
wrapped itself
around your neck.
It will happen again.
It always does.

Waiting Around

The girl thinks
story of my life
when she reads the note
on the refrigerator door.
She wishes there was
an Eskimo Pie in the freezer
but she knows
the chances of that
are negative five hundred.
Here's the entire house:
she could freak out,
blast any music she wants.
They won't be back until late.
It seems like a *Swan Lake* moment.
She puts the music on
and jumps from diningroom to kitchen
to front hall to livingroom.
The audience is whistling and clapping
she bows deeply and modestly
and collapses on the couch
to read the junk mail.

She is reading a catalogue
of camping gear and wondering
why her family didn't wait for her
to get home before they left
for Wisconsin – she likes Wisconsin –
it is one of her favourite places!
That was a lame excuse her mother
had put in the note:
we aren't sure when your class is over.
She practises saying,
'Thanks a lot for
waiting, you guys,'

in a tragic manner
for when they got home.
That would fix them.

Was that a weird noise?
She locks the screen door
in the back and looks out
from the porch
to the lilies-of-the-valley:
Nothing.
The phone is ringing.
She wishes someone else
was here to answer it.
She opens a box of graham crackers
and lets it ring.
It's not for me anyway.
That she knows
from past experience.
Some dum-dum for her brother.
Or one of her aunts or something.
She would like to go
on a bike ride
down to the lake –
only it's Saturday
and it's uncool
not to have a date for tonight.
If she met some jerk from school
they'd know the awful truth
because she didn't seem like
she was getting ready for anything.
When did she start thinking that way?
Janet, from her English class had seen her
one Saturday night at *31 Flavors*
and asked her (sarcastically)
who she was going out with.
She was with her family.
Too bad her face had gone red –

now she knows to stay inside
and avoid all idiots.
What a gyp.
Page 42 of this catalogue
has a nice skirt
she wouldn't mind ordering.
50 dollars – a bargain.

That's when the doorbell rings.
She crawls over to the window
and sees a girl she knows:
Cody Barry – no way!
What does *she* want?
The mail-flap flaps,
then feet down the front steps:
creak, creak, creak, plonk.
In the hallway a little envelope
with her name on it.
Gosh darn it, she thinks,
some dopey birthday party.
The girl reads the corny invitation
and says 'puke' to the empty house.
She sits upside down
on an armchair and looks up
at her legs and feet
trying to figure out
if they are the correct shape.
She thinks the only way
to really judge them
would be if they were attached
to someone else –
she's too used to them.
She tells herself they look OK –
not fabulous, but OK.

Something gives her the creeps
about all these quiet rooms.

What if there is a car accident
and she is the only surviving person
from her whole family
and the TV news crew
comes to film her reaction?
She runs to the big mirror
in her parents' bedroom
for the sorrowful scene.
The girl concentrates hard,
tears form in her eyes.
They drip down her face
and cascade off her jaw.
When she realises what she's doing
she shakes her head
and slaps her cheek:
you rotten, horrible person.

In the drawer to her left
is her mother's make-up collection.
This could be the solution
to her popularity problems!
First, there is something
she needs BADLY: human voices.
After turning on the TV,
she gets two cookies, a fashion magazine
and a glass of Hawaiian Punch
and begins her transformation.
On page 82 it states –
'Pull your hair back neatly
into a pony tail.
Only then can you truly see
the shape of the canvas
you will be painting.
Now decide which category
your face fits: is it square
or round? Are you that lucky girl
with a perfect heart-shaped face?

Or are you more the classic oval?
Now let's look at foreheads –
is yours high or low, narrow or wide?
Is your skin-tone pink or olive,
sallow or pale or combination?'
The girl grabs some eye shadow
and smears it on her eyelids
regardless of colour or shape.
What the hell, she thinks,
since my dumb old face
isn't any shape at all.

While streaking her cheeks
with crimson blush
the girl begins to wonder
why they didn't wait for her.
Odd.
They always waited before.
They knew she wouldn't be very long
at her skating class.
Maybe she's getting too old
for family outings –
more room for everyone else.
'Boy oh boy do I look
like a complete reject', she mutters,
when her new image is finished.
She wishes she knew
how Gina in her civics class
can wear this stuff
and look like Miss Perfect Person
or somebody.
This time she really *does*
hear a noise downstairs.
She glances around quickly
for a weapon – the baseball bat
in the closet.
She tells herself to RELAX:
it's only the TV blasting.

The girl scrubs her face
but her lips keep some red
which she tries to lick off
with her tongue.
It's the taste of school plays:
her mother would tell her
to hold still with
her mouth in an O.
'Close your lips on this tissue' –
a perfect kiss-print.
She doesn't know why she finds
kiss-prints on tissue depressing
but she goes downstairs
and realises it's getting dark.
She wishes life was simple,
like getting nervous
before a big school production –
that was a good feeling.
How does everyone else
know how to do everything,
she wonders, when she can't
figure anything out?

She is hoping some of that
Edwardos pizza is left
from last night –
the girl finds it
and breathes in the smell –
Not Just a Pizza – a Legend.
Things are looking up.
When it's in the oven
and she's leaning on the counter,
reading the history of peanut butter
from the label on a jar of chunky,
she tells herself not to forget
to finish that rotten book-report
for Monday morning.
How sordid!

Some person she doesn't even know
telling her what books
she has to read.
She checks the pizza
and searches around
for the *TV Guide*.
The girl has her head
wedged under the couch
when the phone starts ringing again.
'Blast,' she says, and decides
she'd better answer it after all.
When she hears the voice
on the other end,
she is REALLY sorry she did.
It's her aunt blah, blah, blah,
explaining all about
her cousin boring, boring, boring.
She puts the receiver down
and goes to test the pizza.
She comes back and says,
'Really? Straight A's?'
and resumes her quest
for the *TV Guide*.
The girl thinks, 'What a family!'
as she makes a noise
into the mouthpiece
that sounds semi–interested.
The voice is saying
'and her teachers are begging us
to send her to a school
for gifted pupils,
but I don't really know...'
The girl says, 'Right'
and notices the *TV Guide*
sticking out from under
a cushion nearby.

She doesn't know why
she wonders what's on –
she watches *Saturday Night at the Movies*
every week – no matter what movie it is.
The girl imagines some man
at the network saying,
'Well, let's face it, guys,
we have to schedule a movie
on Saturday night for all those losers
out there with no social life.
It's part of our responsibility.'
Her aunt senses that she
has lost her audience
and sums up with:
'I'll let you go – I bet
you're *real* busy.'
Such wit!
She is standing on the porch
watching the lightning bugs
while chewing onion pizza.
The thing is – she doesn't even
want to go out anywhere.
Why is she such a nudnik?
Why doesn't everyone get off her case?
She laughs at herself
standing there trying to cut
the mozzarella with her teeth
as the strings get longer and longer
the further she pulls the pizza away.
Who invented this stuff, for godsake?
Some joker, no doubt, she thinks
as it snaps and hangs off her mouth.

She hears the front door –
what a relief, they're home!
But when she goes inside
it's her older brother
and his with-it friends.

She is invisible to them.
The girl observes how to be cool.
How silver bracelets
improve your smile.
How to use your teeth.
How to flick your hair around.
How to tell whose father
is a lawyer by the style
of shoes they wear.
All carefully noted.

She bites into the last slice of pizza
before her brother's nose
starts to draw the rest of him
forward to the kitchen.
'Who's that?' a voice asks
and her brother replies:
'My dumb sister' –
exactly the right description.
She goes back to the porch.
The girl has no future plans
except to live in New York
and not be anyone's dumb sister.

The groovy gang inside
have decided what to do
with the rest of the evening
and drift somewhere else.
They have left behind cellophane,
cigarette butts and an aroma
of incense and musk.
It's time to make popcorn
for the movie and to stop feeling
so weird, so nervous.

As she shakes the kernels in the pan
over the gas ring she thinks
how she'll probably end up
just like this stuff:
pop all of a sudden
into a real live person.
It's just this waiting around
for it to happen
that drives her nutty.